Origins

I'm the Leader!

Tony Bradman ✖ Jonatronix

OXFORD

UNIVERSITY PRESS

In this story ...

Max

Cat

Ant

Tiger

2

Also in this story ...

Magpies are easy to spot with their black and
white feathers. They are omnivorous
(*say* om-niv-er-us) which means
they eat all kinds of food.
Magpies like to collect
objects, especially
shiny things.

magpie

Chapter 1 – Max loses his temper

The trouble started as soon as Tiger got to the micro-den.

"You're late, Tiger," Max said, "as usual." Tiger opened his mouth to reply. Max held his hand up. "Never mind the excuses. I've got a job for you …"

"No, thanks," said Tiger, scowling at him. "*Your* jobs are always boring! I'm fed up with you telling us what to do. Who made *you* the leader?"

"We all kind of agreed," said Ant.

"Well, maybe it's time for a change," snapped Tiger.

"Oh, I get it!" said Max. He was scowling now, too. "*You* want to be the leader! I should have known."

Soon the two boys were shouting at each other.

"Hey, calm down!" said Cat.

Ant also tried to stop Max and Tiger arguing. It was no use. They were not listening.

"I've had enough of this," yelled Max at last. "You be the leader if you want to. I won't stay where I'm not wanted." He turned and stomped off without looking back.

Chapter 2 – Carried away!

Tiger watched his friend walk away. "Mr *High and Mighty* Max," he grumbled to himself. "At least we can have some fun now."

"Psst, Ant," Cat whispered. "Do you think Max will be all right?"

"I hope so," said Ant, with a frown. "He told me he was working on a new invention."

"We better stay with Tiger then," said Cat. "To keep him out of trouble. You know what he's like."

"Good idea."

"Hey, are you whispering about me?" said Tiger.

"Not really," said Cat. "We were just wondering what you want to do?"

"Well ..." Tiger stopped to think. "As the leader, I've decided we should play hide and seek in the bushes by the pond."

Cat and Ant followed Tiger out of the micro-den.

They had not gone very far when they saw a shiny piece of metal.

"It's a ring pull from a can," said Cat. She picked it up. "Somebody must have dropped it. Let's find a bin."

Suddenly a shadow fell over them. Tiger looked up and saw a huge bird swooping down.

"Magpie!" Tiger yelled.

"Run!" said Ant.

The children ran in different directions. The magpie squawked and beat its wings. It flew after Cat and grabbed her in its claws. Cat screamed as it took off into the air.

Arrggghhh!

Meanwhile ...

Max had been feeling bad for shouting at
Tiger. He wanted to make it up to his friend.

"Wait till he sees this," Max said to himself.
"He'll forget about our argument."

Max flicked a switch on his new invention.
The micro-machine purred into life ... and
hovered in the air.

Chapter 3 – Tiger's plan

"It must have been the ring pull!" gasped Ant. "Magpies like shiny things."

"What shall we do?" asked Tiger.

"You're the leader, Tiger. *You* think of something!"

"Oh, yeah ... right," said Tiger. He suddenly wished Max was there. Max would know what to do. He would think of something like ...

"The micro-copter!" Tiger said. He turned to Ant. "You stay here and watch where the magpie takes Cat. I'll be back in a minute."

Tiger ran as fast as he could back to the micro-den. Moments later he was strapped into the micro-copter. Tiger hit the start button.

Tiger felt his stomach lurch as he rose into the air. He quickly flew back to Ant.

Ant pointed to a nearby tree. "Up there," he called.

Tiger steered carefully between the tangled branches. He saw Cat's yellow jumper through the green leaves.

"Help!" Cat shouted, when she saw him.

The nest was full of shiny things the magpie had taken. But the magpie was nowhere to be seen.

"Are you OK?" Tiger asked.

"Yes," said Cat, shakily. "But I thought that bird was going to eat me!"

"Nah … You would probably give it tummy ache!" smiled Tiger.

Cat scowled at him.

Just then, there was a crashing noise. The whole nest shook.

The magpie was back. It landed on the edge of the nest. It stared at them with its beady, black eyes.

Chapter 4 – The new invention

"Do something, Tiger!" yelped Cat, backing away from the bird.

But Tiger's mind was like a clean whiteboard. All he could do was stare at the magpie's beak and claws. They looked *very* sharp. He knew Cat was depending on him. He realized that being leader was not as easy as he had thought.

It was then Cat heard a humming noise.
She peeked over the edge of the nest.

"Max —" said Cat.

"Yes, I wish he was here, too," said Tiger sadly.

"He is!" she gasped.

Just then a silver and blue shape zoomed
past them.

The magpie squawked angrily. It flapped its wings and took off after the speeding shape.

The shape zoomed back again and stopped. Max was standing on a hover board ... in mid-air! The hover board was sleek, shiny and incredibly cool.

"Wow!" Tiger gasped.

Max grinned. His grin faded when he heard the squawking behind him.

"Get Cat out of here," said Max to Tiger. "I'll lead the magpie away." With that, Max darted off.

Tiger started the micro-copter again. It was slower flying with two people. But Cat and Tiger were soon safely back on the ground.

Chapter 5 – Friends again

Cat, Ant and Tiger stared up at the sky until their eyes watered.

"Can anyone see Max?" asked Ant.

"There he is!" said Cat, with relief.

Max landed next to them. "Sorry it took so long. That magpie was difficult to shake off."

"I'm the one who's sorry," said Tiger. "You are a much better leader than me!"

"You weren't that bad!" grinned Max. "Let's take it in turns."

Tiger looked longingly at the hover board.

"That job I wanted you to do earlier ... It was to test the hover board," Max said. "Still want a go?"

Yeah!